DENVER
BRONCOS

BY PATRICK KELLEY

SportsZone

An Imprint of Abdo Publishing
abdopublishing.com

abdopublishing.com

Printed in the United States of America, North Mankato, Minnesota
042016
092016

THIS BOOK CONTAINS
RECYCLED MATERIALS

Cover Photo: Kevin Terrell/AP Images
Interior Photos: Kevin Terrell/AP Images, 1; Gregory Payan/AP Images, 4-5; Charlie Riedel/AP Images, 6; AP Images, 7, 16-17; Rich Clarkson Associates/AP Images, 8-9; NFL Photos/AP Images, 10-11, 12-13; Vernon Biever/AP Images, 14-15; Tony Tomsic/AP Images, 18; Michael S. Green/AP Images, 19; Elise Amendola/AP Images, 20-21; Kevin Terrell/AP Images, 22-23; Ric Tapia/AP Images, 24-25, 26-27, 28-29

Editor: Patrick Donnelly
Series Designer: Nikki Farinella

Cataloging-in-Publication Data
Names: Kelley, Patrick, author.
Title: Denver Broncos / by Patrick Kelley.
Description: Minneapolis, MN : Abdo Publishing, [2017] | Series: NFL up close | Includes index.
Identifiers: LCCN 2015960368 | ISBN 9781680782158 (lib. bdg.) | ISBN 9781680776263 (ebook)
Subjects: LCSH: Denver Broncos (Football team)--History--Juvenile literature. | National Football League--Juvenile literature. | Football--Juvenile literature. | Professional sports--Juvenile literature. | Football teams--Colorado--Juvenile literature.
Classification: DDC 796.332--dc23
LC record available at http://lccn.loc.gov/2015960368

TABLE OF CONTENTS

GOLDEN MOMENT

Denver Broncos linebacker Von Miller raced past the Carolina Panthers' offensive line. He grabbed quarterback Cam Newton and raked the football out of his hands. Miller's teammate, Malik Jackson, fell on the ball in the end zone for a Denver Broncos touchdown.

Miller's big play set the tone for the Broncos' 24-10 victory in Super Bowl 50 on February 7, 2016. Led by star quarterback Peyton Manning and a dominating defense, the Broncos showed they were the best team in football.

Von Miller had a huge game for the Broncos in Super Bowl 50.

At 39 years old, Manning became the oldest quarterback to win a Super Bowl. It was the Denver defense that was truly special, however. It was ranked number one in the National Football League (NFL) for good reason.

Miller and his teammates spent all night in Newton's face. Miller forced two Newton fumbles that led to two Broncos touchdowns. After the game, Miller was named the Super Bowl's Most Valuable Player (MVP).

Von Miller strips the ball from Cam Newton in the second half of Super Bowl 50.

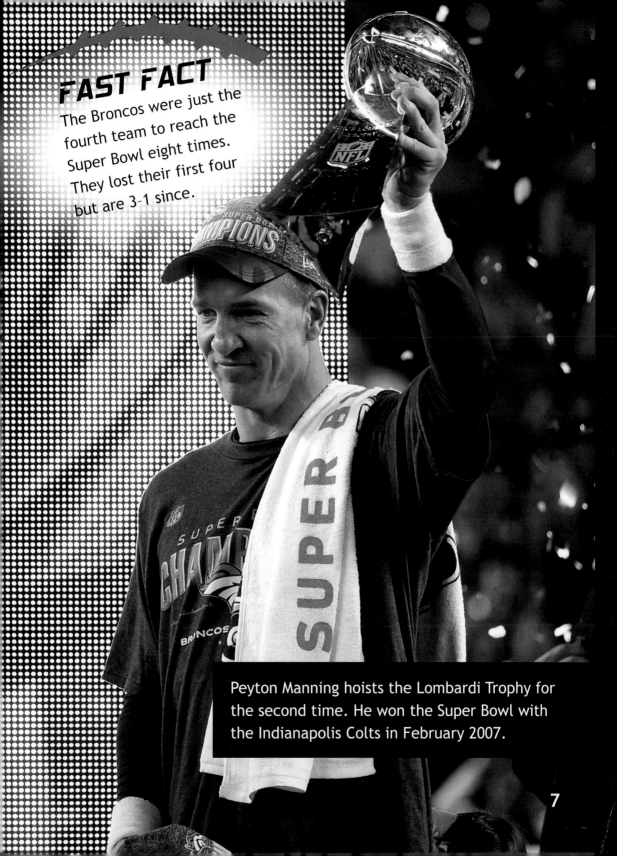

Peyton Manning hoists the Lombardi Trophy for the second time. He won the Super Bowl with the Indianapolis Colts in February 2007.

TOUGH START

The Denver Broncos were one of the original eight teams in the American Football League (AFL). The league began play in 1960 as a challenger to the NFL.

On September 9, 1960, the Broncos played the first game in AFL history. They beat the Boston Patriots 13-10. Although they won that first game, the Broncos struggled in the 1960s. In 10 seasons from 1960 to 1969, they won just 39 games while losing 97 and tying four.

Broncos running back Hewritt Dixon tries to break a tackle against the Kansas City Chiefs in 1963.

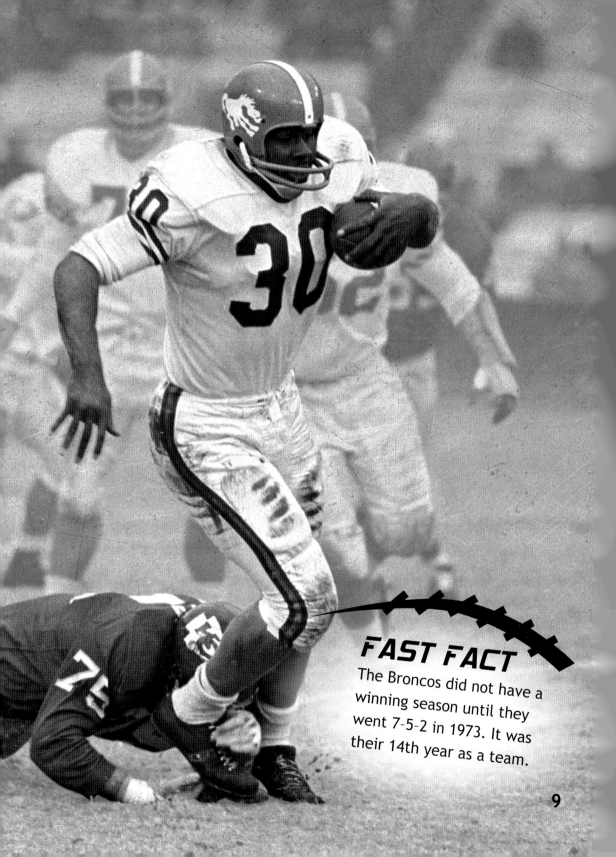

FAST FACT

The Broncos did not have a winning season until they went 7-5-2 in 1973. It was their 14th year as a team.

Floyd Little, *44*, pulls away from two Los Angeles Rams defenders in 1972.

The Broncos did not just struggle on the field. They had a hard time getting fans to the games, too. In fact, the Broncos almost left Denver because they did not have very much support from fans.

Near the end of the 1960s, things started to change. In 1967, the Broncos drafted running back Floyd Little. For the next nine years, Little was one of the best players in professional football. He led the NFL in rushing yards in 1971 and in rushing touchdowns in 1973.

With Little leading the way, the people of Denver started to pay more attention to the Broncos. And in 1970, another big change was in store for the Broncos and the rest of the pro football world.

FAST FACT

Floyd Little was inducted into the Pro Football Hall of Fame in 2010.

BUILDING BLOCKS

At the end of the 1969 season, the AFL completed its merger with the NFL. Three NFL teams joined the 10 former AFL teams to form the American Football Conference (AFC). Soon after, the Broncos finally started winning.

In the 1970s, the Broncos focused on building a tough defense. They were nicknamed the "Orange Crush" after a popular soda, because they wore orange jerseys and so often crushed their opponents. In 1977, the Orange Crush defense led Denver to its best season yet. That year, the Broncos went 12-2 and reached the playoffs for the first time.

FAST FACT

Four members of the Orange Crush defense were named first-team All-Pro in 1977: defensive end Lyle Alzado, linebackers Randy Gradishar and Tom Jackson, and safety Bill Thompson.

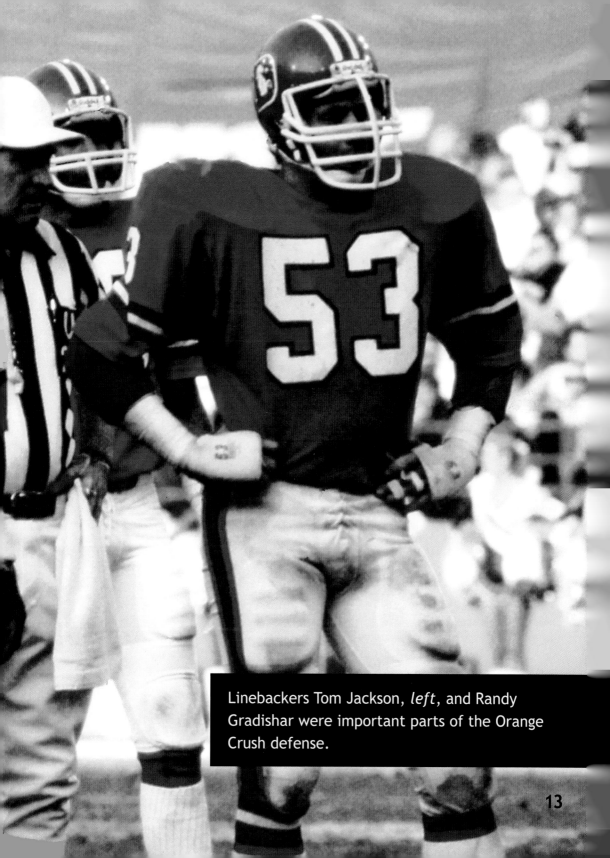

Linebackers Tom Jackson, *left*, and Randy Gradishar were important parts of the Orange Crush defense.

Once they got to the playoffs, the Broncos kept rolling. They beat the mighty Pittsburgh Steelers 34-21. Then they knocked off their division rival Oakland Raiders 20-17 in the AFC Championship Game. The longtime losers were headed to the Super Bowl.

Then the roll ended. The Dallas Cowboys also had gone 12-2 and had beaten the Broncos in the regular season. Denver was overmatched from the start and lost the Super Bowl 27-10. Despite the defeat, the rest of the NFL knew the Broncos were finally contenders.

The Dallas Cowboys' defense hassled Broncos quarterback Craig Morton, *right*, throughout their Super Bowl matchup.

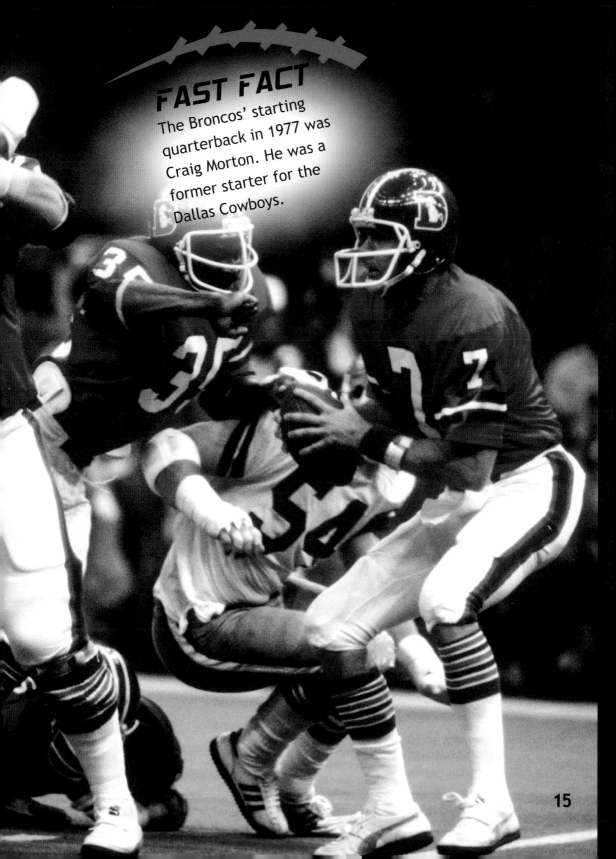

FAST FACT

The Broncos' starting quarterback in 1977 was Craig Morton. He was a former starter for the Dallas Cowboys.

15

BECOMING THE BEST

John Elway looks for an open receiver against the Cleveland Browns in the 1986 AFC Championship Game.

In 1983, the Broncos traded two players and a top draft pick to the Baltimore Colts for the right to sign John Elway. The rookie quarterback with the rocket arm was drafted first overall by the Colts, but he did not want to play in Baltimore. Elway's arrival in Denver changed the Broncos forever.

By his fourth season, Elway had led Denver back to the Super Bowl. But the Broncos lost. Then they lost two more Super Bowls in the next three seasons. Each loss was worse than the previous one. The New York Giants beat them 39-20. Then the Broncos lost to Washington 42-10. Finally, the San Francisco 49ers humiliated Denver 55-10. People began to wonder if Elway would ever win a title.

FAST FACT

John Elway drove the Broncos 98 yards for a touchdown to send the 1986 AFC Championship Game into overtime. Denver went on to beat the Cleveland Browns 23-20.

The question seemed to nag the Broncos, too. Over the next six seasons, they missed the postseason four times and won only one playoff game. In 1996, the Broncos went 13-3 and had the top seed in the AFC playoffs. But they lost at home to the Jacksonville Jaguars, a team that had been in the NFL for only two seasons.

Elway turned 37 before the 1997 season. Time was running out. But he was about to write a storybook ending to his legendary career.

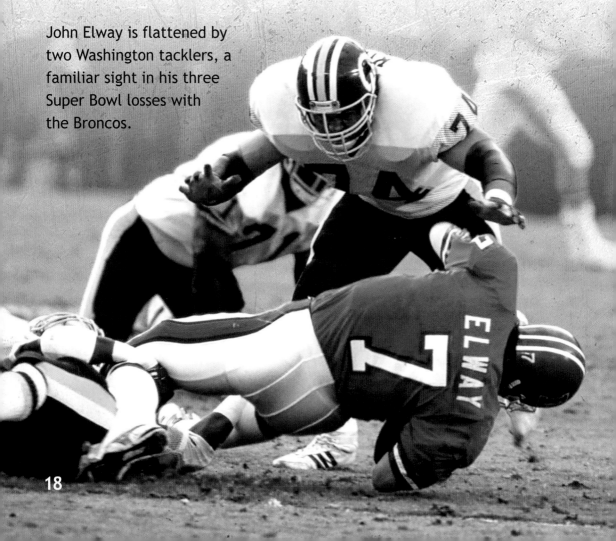

John Elway is flattened by two Washington tacklers, a familiar sight in his three Super Bowl losses with the Broncos.

John Elway looks dejected as the Broncos lose to the Jacksonville Jaguars in the 1996 AFC playoffs.

Terrell Davis ripped through the Green Bay
defense in his Super Bowl MVP performance.

The Broncos earned a wild card spot in the 1997 playoffs. Then they won two tough road games to get back to the Super Bowl. The defending champion Green Bay Packers were waiting for them. Elway was able to lean on his defense and running game that day. The Broncos forced three turnovers. Running back Terrell Davis rushed for 157 yards and three touchdowns. The Broncos won 31-24. At age 37, Elway had his Super Bowl ring.

But he was not finished. Saving his best for last, Elway led the Broncos back to the Super Bowl after the 1998 season. In his last NFL game, Elway won the Super Bowl MVP Award as the Broncos beat the Atlanta Falcons 34-19.

During Elway's 16 seasons as the Broncos' starting quarterback, the team reached the playoffs 10 times and played in five Super Bowls.

He did not do it alone, of course. The Broncos had many great players on the team during their championship years. Tight end Shannon Sharpe was one of the best to ever play his position. Wide receivers Rod Smith and Ed McCaffrey were two of Elway's favorite targets. Davis was the MVP of their first Super Bowl win. He won the NFL MVP Award when he rushed for 2,008 yards and 21 touchdowns the next year.

Rod Smith hauls in an 80-yard touchdown pass from John Elway against the Atlanta Falcons in the Super Bowl.

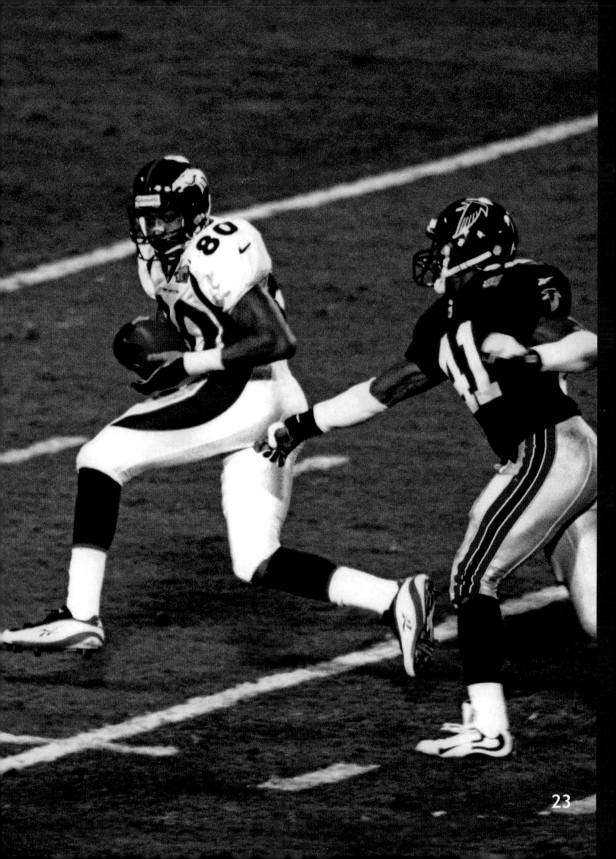

MANNING'S RIDE

The Broncos hit a bit of a slump after John Elway retired. In the next 12 seasons, they made the playoffs just four times and won one playoff game. Elway returned to the Broncos in 2011 but not as a quarterback. He was hired as the general manager. That means he was responsible for building a winning team. And that is exactly what he did.

The Broncos won the AFC West division in each of Elway's first five years as general manager, 2011 to 2015. No surprise for a great quarterback, his biggest move was to bring another legendary quarterback to Denver.

As general manager, John Elway, *left*, played a big role in bringing Peyton Manning to Denver.

In 2012, Elway signed free agent quarterback Peyton Manning to a contract. Manning was a star for the Indianapolis Colts for 13 years. But in 2012, he was 36 years old and recovering from a neck injury. The Broncos decided to give him a chance.

What a chance it was, too. In 2012, Manning bounced back and led the Broncos to a 13-3 record. He was even better in 2013. Every pass seemed to find a receiver. His 5,477 passing yards and 55 passing touchdowns were NFL records. However, Denver lost 43-8 to the Seattle Seahawks in the Super Bowl.

Eric Decker, *87*, Demaryius Thomas, *88*, and Wes Welker, *83*, line up against the Baltimore Ravens in 2013.

FAST FACT

Four Broncos caught at least 10 touchdown passes in 2013: wide receivers Demaryius Thomas, Eric Decker, and Wes Welker, and tight end Julius Thomas.

In four seasons with Manning, the Broncos went 50-14. But by 2015, Denver's defensive players had become the stars. Linebacker Von Miller, cornerback Chris Harris Jr., and defensive end DeMarcus Ware gave Denver a defense that was tough to beat. First-year coach Gary Kubiak and the Broncos proved in the Super Bowl against the Carolina Panthers that they could win a championship with a defense that strong.

Broncos defensive end DeMarcus Ware and coach Gary Kubiak celebrate their Super Bowl victory over the Carolina Panthers.

TIMELINE

1960

As one of the original eight members of the AFL, the Denver Broncos play their first season.

1977

In their 17th season, the Broncos finally play a postseason game, defeating the Pittsburgh Steelers 34-21 at Denver's Mile High Stadium on Christmas Eve.

1983

The Broncos trade for rookie quarterback John Elway.

1987

On January 11, Elway engineers "The Drive" to beat the Cleveland Browns, 23-20, in the AFC Championship.

1990

The Broncos play in their third Super Bowl in four years on January 28. They lose 55-10 to the San Francisco 49ers.

1998

Elway and Terrell Davis lead the Broncos to a 31-24 win against the Green Bay Packers on January 25, giving Denver its first Super Bowl victory.

1999

On January 31, John Elway leads the Broncos to a 34-19 Super Bowl win against the Atlanta Falcons in his final NFL game.

2014

Back in the Super Bowl for the first time in 15 years, the Broncos lose to the Seattle Seahawks 43-8 on February 2.

2016

On February 7, Denver's defense smothers the Carolina Panthers as the Broncos win Super Bowl 50, 24-10.

GLOSSARY

COORDINATOR
An assistant coach who is in charge of a team's offense or defense.

DRAFT
The process by which leagues determine which teams can sign new players coming into the league.

FUMBLE
When a player with the ball loses possession, allowing the opponent a chance to recover it.

MERGE
Join with another to create something new, such as a company, a team, or a league.

ROOKIE
A first-year player.

SLUMP
A period of time when a player or team is not doing well.

TURNOVER
Loss of the ball to the other team through an interception or fumble.

INDEX

ABOUT THE AUTHOR

Patrick Kelley is a freelance writer based in Denver, Colorado. He has been a sports journalist for nearly 20 years and has written dozens of books about sports and two about American history. A native of Colorado, he lives with his wife and four children in his home state.